SCIENCE
MAGIC
WITH SOUND

CHRIS OXLADE

BARRON'S

JERSEY

First edition for the United States, Canada, and the Philippines published 1994 by Barron's Educational Series, Inc.

Design
David West Children's Book Design
Designer
Steve Woosnam-Savage
Editor
Suzanne Melia
Illustrator
Ian Thompson
Photographer
Roger Vlitos

© Aladdin Books Ltd. 1993
Created and designed by
N.W. Books
28 Percy Street
London W1P 9FF

First published in
Great Britain in 1993 by
Franklin Watts Ltd.
96 Leonard Street
London EC2A 4RH

All inquiries should be addressed to:
Barron's Educational Series, Inc.
250 Wireless Boulevard
Hauppauge, NY 11788

International Standard Book No.
0-8120-6446-1 (hardcover)
0-8120-1985-7 (paperback)

Library of Congress Catalog
Card No. 94-5550

Library of Congress Cataloging-in-Publication Data

Oxlade, Chris.
Science magic with sound / Chris Oxlade. — 1st ed. for the U.S., Canada, and the Philippines.
p. cm. — (Science magic)
Includes index.
ISBN 0-8120-6446-1. — ISBN 0-8120-1985-7 (pbk.).
1. Conjuring–Juvenile literature.
2. Sound—Juvenile literature. 3. Scientific recreations—Juvenile literature. [1. Magic tricks. 2. Sound. 3. Scientific recreations.]
I. Title. II. Series.
GV1548.O97 1994   94-5550
793.8—dc20   CIP
                                                    AC

Printed in Belgium
4567 4208 987654321

CONTENTS

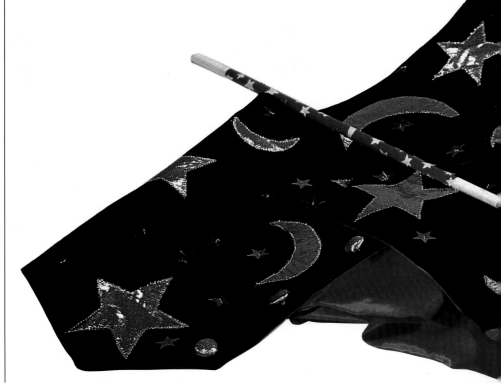

SOUND MAGIC!

Imagine what it's like in outer space where there is no sound at all! This is so because sound needs to travel through a gas such as air, a liquid such as water, or a solid such as wood. Even though we cannot see sound, our ears can tell us where sounds are coming from. But can we always believe our ears? Sound is a natural trickster that can change direction, become quieter or louder, and even make objects move without being touched. Sounds like magic!

BE AN EXPERT MAGICIAN

PREPARING YOUR ROUTINE

There is much more to being a magician than just doing tricks. It is important that you and your assistant practice your whole routine lots of times, so that your performance goes smoothly when you do it for an audience. You will be a more entertaining magician if you do.

PROPS

Props are all the bits and pieces of equipment that a magician uses during an act, including his or her clothes as well as the things needed for the tricks themselves. It's a good idea to make a magician's trunk from a large box to keep all your props in. During your routine, you can dip into the trunk, pulling out all sorts of crazy objects (see Misdirection). You could also tell jokes about these objects.

PROPS LIST

Magic wand ★ Top hat ★ Vest ★ Ball Balloons ★ Bottles with lids ★ Cardboard boxes of various sizes ★ Cardboard tubes ★ Cassette player with headphones and tapes ★ Cellophane tape Cloths ★ Colored paper ★ Colored silk scarves Curtains ★ Decorated backdrop ★ Egg cartons or trays Glass jars, some with lids ★ Glove puppet ★ Glue ★ Music box mechanism ★ Oil-based paints ★ Old candle ★ Plastic tubing ★ Playing cards Scissors ★ Small radio ★ Sticky putty ★ String ★ Thin cardboard, white and colored ★ Tissue paper ★ Water ★ Wine glasses ★ Yogurt containers

WHICH TRICKS?

Work out which tricks you want to put in your routine. Include some long tricks and some short tricks to keep your audience interested. If you can, include a trick that you can keep going back to during the routine. Magicians call this a "running gag."

MAGICIAN'S PATTER

Patter is what you say during your routine. Good patter makes a routine much more interesting and allows it to run more smoothly. It is a good way to entertain your audience during the

slower parts of your routine. Try to make up a story for each trick. Remember to introduce yourself and your assistant at the start and to thank the audience at the end. Practice your patter when you practice your tricks.

MISDIRECTION

Misdirection is an important part of a magician's routine. By waving a colorful scarf in the air or telling a joke, you can distract an audience's attention from something you'd rather they didn't see!

KEEP IT SECRET

The best magicians never give away their secrets. If anyone asks how your tricks work, just reply, "By magic!" Then you can impress people with your tricks again and again.

INTRODUCING MAGIC MELISSA
AND THE
AMAZING VACUUM JAR

How is it possible? Magic Melissa silences music simply by sucking up through the tube!

Lower your music box mechanism into the jar, making sure that it does not touch the sides. Now stretch the balloon over the top of the jar to seal the opening. The audience will still be able to hear the music. Now suck as much air as you can from the jar. Squeeze the neck of the balloon between sucks to keep the vacuum. The sound will gradually fade.

WHAT YOU NEED
*Thin cardboard
Scissors ★ Large glass
jar ★ Plastic tubing
String ★ Music box
mechanism (or small
radio) ★ Balloon*

THE SCIENCE
BEHIND THE TRICK

When you speak, you make the tiny particles (called molecules) that make up air vibrate. The vibrations are passed from one molecule to the next, spreading the sound. Your ear detects the vibrating air so that you can hear sound. In a vacuum, however, there is no air, so sound cannot travel. When you first put the music box mechanism into the jar, the sound can travel through the air inside. But when you suck, there is less air in the jar. The sound cannot travel as well and therefore grows fainter.

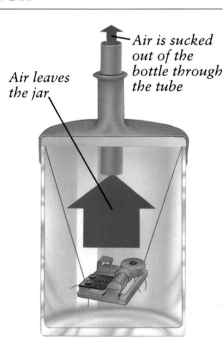

Air is sucked out of the bottle through the tube

Air leaves the jar

2 Pierce two holes in the cardboard disc, and use the string to attach the music box mechanism.

1 Cut a circle of cardboard to fit exactly over the top of your glass jar. Cut a small hole in the center of the circle just large enough for the plastic tubing to fit through.

3 Cut off the lower part of a balloon and push the neck over a length of plastic tubing.

INTRODUCING MAGIC MOLLY
AND THE
MAGIC GLASSES

Magic Molly makes a glass sing and the playing card moves mysteriously.

WHAT YOU NEED
Deck of playing cards
Two identical wine glasses ★ Water

Put the two wine glasses (with the water already in them) on the table, about 2 in. (5 cm) apart. Ask a volunteer to pick a card from the deck. Put the remaining cards under the edge of one of the glasses, and rest the selected card on top of the tilted glass. Now wet your finger in the other glass, and run it around the rim. The glass will sing and the card will begin to move!

THE SCIENCE BEHIND THE TRICK

Running your wet finger around the glass makes the glass vibrate, producing a ringing sound. The pitch of the sound (the note it makes) depends on the level of water. When the sound reaches the other glass, it also vibrates. Because the level of the water is the same, the second glass picks up the vibrations well. This effect is called *resonance*. The vibrations make the card on top of the glass slide.

Sound waves travel through the air

When the sound waves reach the second glass, it also vibrates

As the glass is rubbed it vibrates, producing sound waves

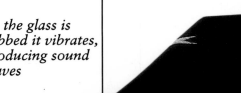

1 This is a very easy trick to prepare for! First, find a deck of playing cards and two identical wine glasses.

2 Before you perform your routine, fill both wine glasses about half full of water. Make sure that the level of water is the same in both glasses.

INTRODUCING MAGIC MOLLY
AND THE
HEARING HAT

The amazing hearing hat brings music to Magic Molly's ears!

WHAT YOU NEED
Large sheet of thin
colored cardboard
Scissors ★ Glue
Plastic tubing ★ Colored
paper or paints
Cassette player with
headphones and tapes

Put on the hearing hat before you start the trick. Ask a volunteer from the audience to secretly select one of the tapes, put it into the cassette player, and press the PLAY button. Nobody will be able to hear the music. Take off your hat, put it over the headphones, listen, and then tell the audience which tape is being played!

THE SCIENCE
BEHIND THE TRICK

The sound that comes out of the small speakers in the headphones is very faint. As it spreads out from the headphones, only a tiny bit reaches your ears. When you put the hat over the headphones, the sound that you would not normally hear is collected in the hat and funneled into your ear. As a result you can hear the music better.

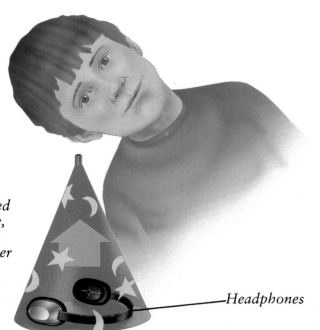

Sound waves are concentrated by the cone, making the sound louder by the time it reaches the top

Headphones

2 Cut off the tip of the cone, and glue in a short piece of the plastic tubing. Using colored paper or paints, decorate the cone with magic symbols to complete the hat.

1 Roll up the large sheet of cardboard to make a cone shape, and trim around the bottom.

INTRODUCING MAGIC MONA
AND THE
TALKING PUPPET

The puppet comes to life as Magic Mona conjures up a voice all its own.

WHAT YOU NEED
Cardboard tubes
Cellophane tape
Balloon ★ Plastic tubing
Scissors ★ Thin
cardboard ★ Decorated
backdrop ★ Glove
puppet ★ Silk scarf

Have the backdrop and tube set up before you start the trick. Your assistant sneaks behind the curtain to operate the glove puppet. Now you can have a conversation with the puppet — and the puppet will talk in your voice! Each time you want the puppet to speak, talk into the end of the tube. You can disguise the tube by covering the end with a silk scarf, and pretending to talk into it. This is an opportunity for some good patter.

THE SCIENCE
BEHIND THE TRICK

When an object makes a sound, it causes the air around it to vibrate. The vibrations (or waves) spread out in all directions. Our ears detect the sound and the direction from which it is coming. When you speak into the tube, however, the sound waves cannot spread out. They bounce down the tube and come out of the cone at the end. Your voice seems to come from the puppet.

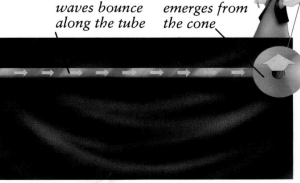

The sound waves bounce along the tube

The sound emerges from the cone

1 Join the cardboard tubes together with the cellophane tape to make a long tube. Cut off the lower part of the balloon and push the neck over a piece of plastic tubing. Attach the balloon to one end of the tubes.

2 On the other end of the tube, attach a cone made from the thin cardboard.

3 Hang a backdrop across your stage as shown and hang the tube behind it.

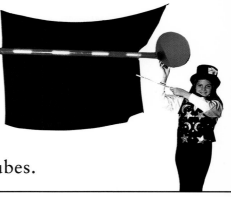

INTRODUCING MAGIC MIRANDA
AND THE
PICK THE CARD TRICK

Magic Miranda stuns her audience by guessing the card correctly every time!

Ask your assistant to tie the blindfold around your head, and sit down at the table. Now ask a volunteer to point to one of the cards on the board. Pretend to concentrate, laying your head on the table. Your assistant now secretly taps the table the correct number of times to indicate which card has been chosen. Call out the card!

WHAT YOU NEED
Deck of playing cards
Sticky putty ★ Colored
cardboard ★ Silk scarf

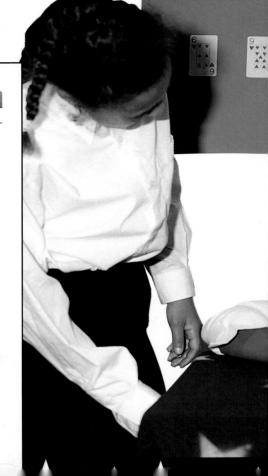

THE SCIENCE
BEHIND THE TRICK

We normally think of sound as traveling through the air. However, it also travels through liquids and solids. In fact, sound travels much better in liquids and solids than it does in air. The tapping is too low to be heard through the air by the audience, but you can hear the sound easily through the solid wood of the table.

The tapping sound travels through the table to your ear

1 Take ten cards
   from the deck of
   playing cards — ace
   (1), 2, 3, and so on.
   Using sticky putty,
   attach the cards to
   a piece of the
   cardboard in two
   rows of five each.

2 Make a blindfold from the colored
   silk scarf. Make sure the audience
   knows you can't see the cards.

INTRODUCING MAGIC MOLLY
AND THE
TELEPORTING TRICK

Magic Molly transports her assistant from one side of the stage to the other.

Hang two curtains at the back of your stage. Now send your assistant behind the left curtain and talk to him or her so that the audience can hear a voice. Now announce that you have transported your assistant to behind the other curtain. Talk to him or her again. This time your assistant's voice appears to come from behind the other curtain — teleported!

WHAT YOU NEED
Scissors ★ Glue ★ Large cardboard box ★ Papier-mâché ★ String ★ Old candle ★ Yogurt containers ★ Colored paper ★ Egg cartons or trays ★ Two curtains

THE SCIENCE
BEHIND THE TRICK

When your assistant speaks into the yogurt container of the string telephone, his or her voice makes the bottom of the container vibrate. The vibrations travel along the taut string and come out of the cone at the other end. The egg cartons in the box absorb your assistant's voice.

The vibrations caused by the sound of a voice travel down the string and emerge at the other end

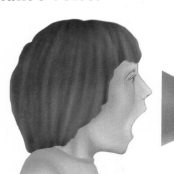

1 Cut off or glue down the flaps of the large cardboard box. Line the inside of the box with the egg cartons or trays.

Thread the string through a yogurt container and tie a knot inside. Pierce a hole in the back of the box, push the loose end of the string through, and add the second container. Glue on a paper cone.

2 Wax a long string by pulling an old candle along it.

INTRODUCING MAGIC MOLLY
AND THE
FIND THE BALL TRICK

Which jar is the ball in? Magic Molly can tell by tapping with her magic wand!

Arrange the three jars in a row on the table and remove the lids. Now ask for a volunteer. With your back turned, ask him or her to place the ball in one of the jars and then put on all the lids. Now tap each jar in turn (to disguise the ringing sounds, say, "Is it in here. . . or here. . . or here?" as you tap). The jar with the odd note is the one that contains the ball.

THE SCIENCE BEHIND THE TRICK

When you strike a jar with your wand, it makes a ringing sound. The pitch of the sound (the sort of note it makes) depends on the size of the jar and the amount of water in it. (To see the effect, try tapping a jar as you pour water into it — the note will gradually get higher.) When the ball is put into a jar, it will sink and make the water level rise, changing the note.

The ball changes the level of the water

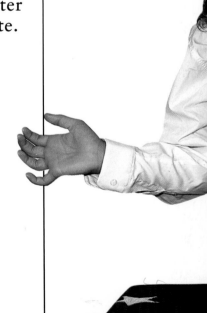

20

1 The three identical glass jars need to be large enough for the ball to fit into. Paint all the jars with the oil-based paint so that you can't see through the glass.

2 Fill each jar half-full of water. The level of water in the jars must be the same (you can make sure that you put the same amount of water in each jar by using a measuring cup). Finally, find a ball that will sink in water.

INTRODUCING MAGIC MAX
AND THE
WHISPERING BOX

The box is empty — so where are the strange whispering sounds coming from?

Start by showing the smaller box to the audience so that they can see that it is empty. Ask for a volunteer to come forward and listen to the box — there will be silence, of course! Now put the smaller box on top of the larger box. Ask your volunteer to listen again by putting an ear against the box. There will be a quiet whispering from inside!

WHAT YOU NEED
Small radio ★ Two cardboard boxes Papier-mâché ★ Tissue paper ★ Cloths Scissors ★ Thin cardboard ★ Cellophane tape ★ Egg cartons or trays

THE SCIENCE
BEHIND THE TRICK

The egg cartons, tissue paper, and cloths absorb the sound coming from the radio. (Soundproof rooms often have egg-carton-like walls.) Some sound, however, travels up the tube and makes the smaller box vibrate, so the radio can be heard when you put your ear to the box.

Sound waves travel up the tube and are amplified by the smaller box

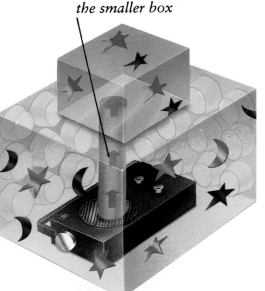

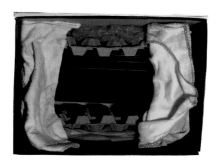

1 Put the radio inside the larger box with the speaker pointing upward. Pack the egg cartons, tissue paper, and cloths around it, but don't cover the speaker.

2 Cut a rectangle of cardboard to fit inside the larger box, and make a cardboard tube to go through the middle of the rectangle as shown.

3 Put the rectangle into the box so that the bottom of the tube touches the speaker. Cut a hole in the box for the tube to poke through.

INTRODUCING MAGIC MELISSA
AND THE
AMPLIFYING BOX

Magic Melissa turns up the volume without ever touching the radio dial!

WHAT YOU NEED
Thin cardboard
Scissors ★ Cellophane
tape ★ Cardboard box
Tissue paper ★ Glue
Small radio

Put the radio on the table, turn it on and adjust the volume so that the sound is quite low. Now announce that you can make the sound louder or softer without touching the radio. Put the box in front of the radio, first with the big hole next to it, then with the small hole next to it. The sound will get louder and then softer!

THE SCIENCE BEHIND THE TRICK

When the box is not in front of the radio, the sound from the speaker spreads out. The audience, sitting in front of the radio, hears only a small amount of the sound. With the box positioned in front as shown, the cone collects the sound and sends it all toward the audience. This makes the radio sound louder as the cone collects and focuses the sound.

The sound is collected and directed toward the audience

2 Cut two holes (one large and one small) in opposite sides of the box. Cover the entire box with the tissue paper to hide the holes.

3 Tape the cone inside the box over the holes.

1 From the thin cardboard, make a cone that will fit inside the box. Snip off the top to make a hole at the narrow end.

INTRODUCING MAGIC MERVYN
AND THE
DISAPPEARING WATER

It doesn't matter which of Magic Mervyn's bottles the audience chooses — it's always empty!

Before the trick, attach the small bottle of water to your right arm with the cellophane tape. Shake one bottle with your left hand — it will sound empty. Shake the other with your right — it will sound full! Mix up the two bottles. Now ask a volunteer to predict which of the bottles is full. Pick up the chosen bottle with your left hand and shake it — it will sound empty.

WHAT YOU NEED
Two identical, medium-sized bottles ★ Oil-based paint ★ A small bottle with lid ★ Water Cellophane tape

THE SCIENCE
BEHIND THE TRICK

Our ears are very good at picking up sound, and can work out approximately where sound is coming from — but not exactly. When you shake the empty bottle in your right hand, the water in the bottle up your sleeve makes a sloshing noise. Because the noise comes from almost where the members of the audience expect it to, they do not suspect anything.

Bottle of water is hidden on the right arm

1 Clean the two identical medium-sized bottle and remove any labels. Paint them with the oil-based paint so that you cannot see inside, and put on their lids.

2 Find a small bottle that you can hide up your sleeve. Half-fill it with water, and put on the lid.

HINTS AND TIPS

Here are some hints and tips for making your props. Good props will make your act look more professional, so spend time making and decorating your props, and look after them carefully. As well as the special props you need for each trick, try to make some general props such as a vest and a magic wand.

Decorate your props with magic shapes cut from colored paper. Paint bottles and tubes with oil-based paint.

You will need cellophane tape and glue to make props. Double-sided tape may also be useful. You can use sticky putty or special plastic sealant to make waterproof joints.

Try cutting magic shapes out of cardboard and using the holes to make stencils.

Your act will look more professional if you make a stage setting. This is easy if you have a backdrop to hang behind the stage. A large piece of black cloth is most effective. Use silver paint to create stars and moons. Decorate pieces of cloth to throw over your table. The overall effect will be dramatic, creating an atmosphere of mystery and magic.

Make your own magician's clothes. Try to find an old hat and vest to decorate. If you can find some silvery material, cut out stars and moons and sew them on. An alternative is to use sequins or anything else that is shiny and dramatic so you look professional.

Table

Backdrop

Cloth

Assistant's table

Make a magician's table by draping a cloth over an ordinary table. You can put the props out of sight underneath.

GLOSSARY

AMPLIFY To make sound louder by using a sound box or cone.

MOLECULES The tiny particles of which substances are made.

PITCH The highness or lowness of a sound. Pitch depends on the frequency of the vibration causing the sound.

RESONANCE The effect produced when a sound makes an object with the same natural frequency of vibration produce a sound.

SOUND WAVES A regular pattern of changes in the pressure of molecules in a solid, liquid, or gas.

SOUNDPROOFING The muffling of sound by materials that bounce it in all directions. A room or box can be soundproofed.

VIBRATION A rapid movement back and forth, causing a sound.

INDEX